'F' BATTERY

ROYAL HORSE ARTILLERY

A SKETCH OF THE HISTORY

OF

'F' BATTERY

ROYAL HORSE ARTILLERY

Major-General F. W. Stubbs
Major A. S. Tyndale-Biscoe

The Naval & Military Press Ltd

published in association with

FIREPOWER
The Royal Artillery Museum
Woolwich

Published by
The Naval & Military Press Ltd
Unit 10 Ridgewood Industrial Park,
Uckfield, East Sussex,
TN22 5QE England
Tel: +44 (0) 1825 749494
Fax: +44 (0) 1825 765701
www.naval–military-press.com

in association with

FIREPOWER
The Royal Artillery Museum, Woolwich
www.firepower.org.uk

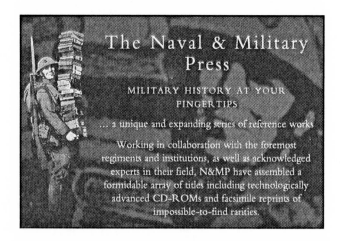

In reprinting in facsimile from the original, any imperfections are inevitably reproduced and the quality may fall short of modern type and cartographic standards.

MONUMENT AT DUM DUM.

Erected to the Memory of the Officers, N.C.O.s, and men of the 1st Troop
1st Brigade Bengal Horse Artillery, who fell in the retreat from Kabul, 1842.

A SKETCH OF THE HISTORY

OF

'F' BATTERY
ROYAL HORSE ARTILLERY

FORMER TITLES

1ST TROOP, 1ST BRIGADE, BENGAL HORSE ARTILLERY
'A' BATTERY, 2ND ROYAL HORSE BRIGADE
'A' BATTERY, 'B' BRIGADE, ROYAL HORSE ARTILLERY

COMPILED FROM NOTES BY

MAJOR-GENERAL F. W. STUBBS

LATE ROYAL ARTILLERY

AND FROM BATTERY RECORDS BY

MAJOR A. S. TYNDALE-BISCOE, R.H.A.

1905

ILLUSTRATIONS

A SKETCH

OF THE

HISTORY OF 'F' BATTERY

ROYAL HORSE ARTILLERY

TOWARDS the end of the year 1800 orders were given for the formation at Dum Dum, in the Presidency of Bengal, of an experimental Brigade of Horse Artillery, at first, of two guns with horse draught. The command was given (G.O. December 4) to Captain-Lieutenant Clement Brown, then Adjutant of the 1st Battalion Bengal Artillery. The guns were brass ones of $4\frac{1}{2}$ cwt.; the carriages $5\frac{1}{2}$ cwt., with beam trails and wheels only $4\frac{1}{2}$ feet in diameter. For these 20 horses were allowed, which were thus disposed :

	Two Guns	One Tumbril	Total
In draught mounted . . .	8	2	10
Two N.C.Os., 4 gunners . .	6	0	6
Spare	2	2	4

The *personnel* was 1 sergeant, 1 corporal, 4 gunners, 8 matrosses. The details were shortly

B

afterwards increased to man six guns. But the Marquess Wellesley, the Governor-General, was very anxious that some Horse Artillery should accompany the force he was sending to Egypt to co-operate with Sir Ralph Abercromby, who was commanding the army operating against Napoleon in that country. His body-guard had galloper guns attached to it; so to avoid delay he supplemented the deficiencies thence, and four guns were sent.

1801. Captain Brown was directed (G.O. February 12) to proceed on this service with the following detail:

—	Captain	Assistant-Surgeon	Conductor	Europeans					Natives				Lascars			Horses	
				Sergeants	Corporals	Farrier	Gunners	Matrosses	Jemadar	Havildars	Naicks	Privates	1st Tindal	2nd Tindals	Lascars		
Horse Artillery .	1	1	1	3	3	1	6	14	—	—	—	—	1	2	40	36	2
Native detail .	—	—	—	—	—	—	—	—	—	2	2	20	—	—	—	—	—
Body-guard .	—	—	—	—	—	—	—	—	1	2	2	22	—	1	11	—	—
	1	1	1	3	3	1	6	14	1	4	4	42	1	3	51	36	2

The remainder were left at Dum Dum under charge, at first, of Lieutenant Marmaduke Browne, afterwards of Lieutenant James H. Brooke.

John Allen was appointed Riding-Master, but, as he was wanted at Dum Dum, Sergeant-Major John Jones, 1st Native Cavalry, was sent in his place with the rank of Conductor of Ordnance.

Captain Brown, with his troop, went round to Bombay by sea, where they joined the remainder of the force under Major-General Sir David Baird.

They sailed up the Red Sea as far as Kosseir, where they disembarked, and marched across the desert to Kenneh, on the Nile. The deficiency of water and want of forage, though the country had been carefully explored for wells, made the march very trying for all the troops, and especially fatal to the horses, and by the time the Nile was reached the guns were drawn by camels. The force sailed up the Nile to Ghizeh, opposite Cairo, and was encamped on the island of Roda for nearly three weeks, till ordered up by General Hutchinson to Rosetta in the end of August. Captain Brown was able to replace his cattle with far better horses than they had brought from India; but the French had just then given up Alexandria, the last place held by them in Egypt, so that the Indian contingent had not the glory of competing in the field with Napoleon's troops.

1802. After the peace of Amiens, the Anglo-Indian army was sent back to Hindustan by Suez. Captain Brown, with the experimental brigade, landed at Calcutta on August 4. Lieutenant J. H. Brooke, on handing over to him the details at Dum Dum, was obliged to go home. He had served in the late war with Tipu Sultan, and had been wounded in action at Malavelli on March 27, 1799, and was an officer of distinguished ability.

1803. The troop was now to consist of a captain, 2 subalterns, 4 sergeants, 4 corporals, 10 gunners,

B

2 trumpeters, 40 matrosses, with native details as before; the ordnance, four 6-pounder guns and two 5½-inch howitzers, and 86 horses. Bullocks were added for draught on the line of march, the horses being reserved for action; but this, being inconvenient, was altered, and the horses increased (October 1804) to 120. The subalterns appointed were Henry Stark, who had gone to Egypt with the Foot Artillery, and James Young. It may be stated here that, as there was no allowance made for the Horse Artillery up to 1817, officers appointed thereto continued to be borne on the rolls of the companies to which they belonged. The troop, being now considered sufficiently perfect in drill and equipment, was ordered to Ghazipur, to be brigaded there with the 8th Royal Irish Dragoons and other cavalry regiments; but as a force was being formed to act against Scindiah, the Mahrátá chief of Gwalior, it was sent on to Cawnpore.

1804. In January it went on, and joined Lord Lake at Biana, near Agra. Scindiah had been defeated at Laswari, and Colonel Monson had been detached with a force to co-operate with Colonel Murray, from Bombay, against the other Mahrátá chief, Holkar, who was preparing to invade our territories. But the disastrous retreat of Colonel Monson, and Holkar's advance, called the troop up again from Cawnpore, where it had been sent again, to join the army which was being formed at Sikander, near

Agra. In September Lord Lake followed Holkar to Muttra and reached Delhi on October 18. Holkar's main force went towards the friendly towns of Deeg and Bhurtpore, but he with his light troops and cavalry went northwards. Major-General Fraser was detached towards Deeg, while Lord Lake, with the cavalry, Horse Artillery, and a reserve brigade of infantry, followed Holkar in a series of rapid marches which have become historical. (See Appendix A.)

'Lake, on reaching Aligunj on the morning of November 16, determined to catch up his enemy before he could destroy the place (Fatehgarh), and ordered the cavalry and Horse Artillery to move on again in the evening, leaving Colonel Don with the infantry and Skinner's Irregular Horse to bring on the baggage. As they mounted, the news arrived of Major-General Fraser's victory at Deeg, a happy omen of success. The moon was up, and the night mild and pleasant ; Major Salkeld had good intelligence, and picked up more as they went along. Holkar was said to have been sitting that night at a nách, when, at a late hour, the news of his defeat at Deeg was brought to him, and to have retired to rest without mentioning it to his chiefs. He was probably revolving by what foul atrocities he could compensate himself here before the approach of Lake should warn him to fly. When the night was nearly past, he was alarmed by a not very distant report.

His attendants believed and told him that it was only the usual morning gun that was fired at Fateh-garh. Sharper ears might have told him there was a warning in the direction from which the sound came. The villagers had no guns. It was the explosion of an English ammunition waggon, in which some powder had probably been shaken out among the shot, and waggons do not usually explode at a walk. Holkar, however, believed his servants. Had not his scouts left Lake late in the afternoon in his camp, more than thirty miles off, and resting after a longer march than usual (23 miles)? So he thought no more of it; but the avenger was very close at hand. Round his tent lay his men, with their horses picqueted beside them, and wrapt in their blankets slept unconscious till, as the first grey light of morning appeared, discharges of grape from the Horse Artillery guns told them who had arrived, and they woke to find the dragoons among them; the 8th Royal Irish leading the way. The carnage was considerable, and as the discomfited host fled they were pursued for ten miles in different directions.

'Holkar, convinced with difficulty of the truth, had mounted early in the fray, and fled, not stopping till he was eighteen miles on the way to Mainpuri.

'He left behind him more than three thousand followers, whose bodies strewed the ground; he left, in a death more dishonourable than theirs, the prestige which his remorseless cruelties had raised high in the eyes of the native powers of India; perhaps higher than that of any Mahrátá chieftain since the days of Sivaji. Our loss was only two dragoons killed and about twenty Europeans and natives wounded, and seventy-five horses.'

Lord Lake in his despatch says : ' I have great satisfaction in reporting to your Lordship the very meritorious conduct of Captain Brown and the corps of Horse Artillery under his command, who by the rapidity of their movements were able to do great execution. Captain Brown's great attention in the management of his corps, and his zeal and activity when called into action, have on every occasion merited my best acknowledgements.'

Thence Lord Lake marched, *via* Mainpuri and Etah, to Muttra, a distance of 147 miles, in nine days without a halt. He reached Deeg, the siege of which was in progress, on December 12. It was evacuated on the 25th.

1805. During the siege of Bhurtpore, January 2–April 15, which followed, the cavalry and Horse Artillery covered the attack. A large portion of Holkar's army, chiefly cavalry, were hanging on our rear. They were joined by Amír Khan, a celebrated leader of horse and freebooter. On February 7, with many of Holkar's men, he went off on a plundering expedition towards Rohilkhand. He was followed up by Major-General Smith, the Horse Artillery, and six regiments of cavalry, which kept so close to him that he could effect but little. He was attacked at Afzalgarh on March 2, and dispersed with loss. The guns here were in much peril, for, a body of Rohilla horse charging down, the General ordered the 29th Dragoons in rear of the troops to repel the attack. Consequently, the enemy were upon them as they reformed after passing through the gun intervals, and they were driven back the same way, thus considerably hampering the guns. But Captain George Russel Deare, of the 8th Royal Irish, on the flank, with the instantaneous decision of a good cavalry leader, promptly wheeled his squadron, and charging down the front cleared it completely.

Major-General Smith, having accomplished all he had to do, rejoined Lord Lake on March 23. He had covered between six and seven hundred miles in forty-four days, including eight halts and four days taken up in crossing the river Ganges. The troop was in a healthy condition, both men and horses fit, during this time, as the muster-rolls show. After the army broke up from before Bhurtpore, it proceeded towards Dholpur to watch Scindiah. The troop then returned to Agra by June 3, and was encamped at Sikander with the British cavalry there. In October it joined a force under Lord Lake, as Holkar was again moving forward, this time in the direction of Sikh territory. Paniput and Karnal were passed, Loodiana on December 2, and the army encamped at Rajpur Ghat, on the Bias, on the 9th.

1806. On January 5, a treaty with the Sikhs having been concluded, and Holkar obliged to return, the army began to retrace its steps, keeping Holkar in front, till in April the troop was back in Agra. Captain Brown left sick in December 1805, and was appointed Commissary of Ordnance in Fort William. Captain-Lieutenant Gervaise Pennington succeeded him; he was senior in the regiment to Brown and was promoted captain in March. He thenceforth remained for the rest of his life in the Bengal Horse Artillery, and was identified with it in all its subsequent improvements. He made himself acquainted with its requirements in equipment, armament, and drill, and has justly been called the Father of the Bengal Horse Artillery.

The ordnance of the Horse Artillery was this year fixed at four 6-pounder guns and two 12-pounder howitzers; though not allowed, apparently, one or two more had been taken into use, as the order directs the excess to be returned to the Agra magazine.

1807. It seems also that the method of mounting all horses in draught was not definitely fixed, as G.O., December 20, 1807, which reduced the number of gun lascars to one 1st and one 2nd tindal and 24 lascars, authorised as gun drivers 1 havildar, 1 naick, and 24 privates.

1808. The value of horse batteries had now

become so manifest that the Government, by order dated August 4, directed the formation of three troops as a permanent establishment. Their strength and equipment are detailed in Appendix D. (The ordnance was now to consist of three calibres— two 12-pounders on the right, two 6-pounders on the left, and two 12-pounder howitzers in the centre. The uniform remained nearly the same as first laid down—a helmet with red horsehair plume, which continued in use till mutiny times, though nominally obsolete ; jacket, leather breeches, gloves, cloak, boots and spurs. The helmets do not appear to have been supplied from home till 1809.)   By this arrangement the troop became 1st Troop, Horse Brigade.

1809. Captain Pennington commanded the whole Horse Brigade in addition to his own troop ; Lieutenant Hugh Lyon Playfair, whose name is still represented in the Royal Artillery, was his adjutant.

The number of horses, which had been 163 since July 1808, was reduced to 145.   Captain Pennington had remonstrated then.   Colonel Horsford, the commandant of the Bengal Artillery, had recommended 120 men and 185 horses, but the Auditor-General, representing my Lords of the Treasury, objected even to 145 on the ground of expense, so he recommended him to take what he could get, lest the whole project should fail.

1810.   Captain Pennington set to work to draw up regulations for the drill and discipline of the

Horse Brigade; in this he was much aided by his adjutant, Lieutenant Playfair.

1811. In 1811, G.O. February 15 ordered the three troops to march from Nomillah cantonments, Agra, to Meerut, previously completing themselves from the artillery companies there. They reached Meerut next month, and, as there was then no cantonment there, had to mark out their lines and commence building.

1812. This year, the war with Java being in progress, a corps of artillery was formed by drafts of horses and men from Native cavalry regiments, at the Cadet Barracks at Baraset, near Dum Dum. An officer from each troop was detailed for this service —G. E. Gowan from the 1st troop, H.A.; they were employed in Java from February 1813 till March 1815, but are not recorded in any action.

1813. In October the troop proceeded to Rewari, to join a force under Lieutenant-Colonel Knox intended to operate against the Alwar State. Major Alexander McLeod commanded the artillery, Captain J. H. Brooke, of the 3rd troop, took command of the 1st troop, as Captain Pennington's duties in command of the Horse Brigade kept him at Meerut. The Mewáti tribes of the Alwar State had been giving trouble; they stole fourteen of the troop horses at Kot Kasim, seventeen miles S.S.W. of Rewari, but this was the only casualty. The troop was back in Meerut by December 3.

1814. War having been declared with Nepaul, the 1st and 3rd troops joined the 2nd division of the army under Major-General Sir Robert Gillespie in October. They went from Saharanpur to the Dera Dhun, where a Gurkha outpost was established in the fort of Nálápáni, or Kalanga, under Balbhader Singh. The place was reconnoitred on October 24, but being found too strong, Colonel Mawby, in command, waited for General Gillespie's arrival on the 27th. In his report to the General, Colonel Mawby honourably mentions Captain Rodber and Lieutenants Kennedy and Luxford, of the Horse Artillery.

The assault took place on October 31, but, owing to causes it is not easy now to discover, three of the columns failed to co-operate, and Captain Brutton, at the head of 100 dismounted men of the 8th Royal Irish Dragoons, lost more than half his force killed and wounded. The General went forward with two guns under Lieutenants Kennedy and Napier Campbell, and three companies of the 53rd Regiment. Leaving one gun to cover the advance, Kennedy and the other went on, the 53rd men dragging it, till a turn showed them the fort some fifty yards off, a gun pointing at them through a cut in the wall, matchlocks along the top. The fire was so hot that the men wavered and the General got frantic. Major Ludlow, with several officers and men of the reserve column appearing just then, was ordered to attack to the right, and the Horse Artillerymen to arm themselves with the muskets of the dead. The General then, turning to Lieutenant Kennedy and the rest, exclaimed, ' Come on, my lads ; now, Charles, for the honour of the County Down ! ' only a pace or two forward and he fell with a bullet through his heart. Two sergeants and some Horse Artillerymen carried his body to the rear, and the order to retire was given, but it was not heard in front, and gun and gunners were nearly lost. The casualties in the troop this day were : Killed —Matross William Brannen; Trumpeter John Pook, Matrosses William Guring and Hugh McKennell, wounded. A company of artillery and some heavy guns having arrived, a breaching battery was erected, and on November 27 another assault took place, recording another failure and costing the valuable life of Lieutenant Luxford, of the 3rd troop. The fort was finally evacuated, after a most gallant defence, three days after, the supply of water having been cut off.

The other casualties in the troop in this business were four wounded :

November 26.—Gunner John Holder, Matross John Griffin.

November 28.—Matrosses Thomas Parry and Thomas Edwards.

After this, both troops returned to Meerut.

1816. In July 1816, Brevet Major Pennington, having been promoted to the regimental rank, was succeeded by Captain John Peter Boileau.

The following month, a cadet just arrived from

England was appointed to the 1st troop as Acting Fire-worker, Gervaise Pennington, a nephew of his namesake, and in acknowledgment of the valuable services of Major Pennington.

1817. In February the troop was again called out, for the siege of Háthras, a strong fort between Aligarh and Agra. A large artillery force with sixty-six siege pieces was employed. The 1st, 3rd, and the lately raised Rocket troop, Horse Artillery, were sent. Batteries were marked out on the 21st. and next day Captain-Lieutenant G. E. Gowan was sent with three guns to a village on the right of No. 1 Battery to keep down the enemy's fire with shrapnel. The Rocket troop had its own battery after the town was taken. The 1st and 3rd troops volunteered their services, through Major Pennington, and the six 10-inch mortar battery was made over to them in Artillery Brigade orders of the 26th. Another battery was constructed for them on the north face of the fort, commanded by Major Pennington and Captain-Lieutenant Gowan. On March 2 all the batteries opened their renewed fire at 9 A.M. and continued till the principal magazine blew up, and after that till dark, when the place was in our hands. Sir John Horsford, in the last order dictated by him, spoke highly of Major Pennington and of the spirit and conduct of the Horse Artillery. The troop then returned to Meerut.

Again in November the troop was called out for

service. The Mahrátá Pindári war had begun.
The three Horse Artillery troops and the Rocket
troop were attached to the centre (1st) division of
the Grand Army, with which was the Governor-
General. It was formed at Sikandra, Cawnpore
district, and moved to Mahewa, south-east of
Gwalior, on the river Sind, on November 7. The
presence of a formidable force so near overawed
Scindiah, who signed the treaty presented to him.
But a more formidable enemy was encountered; for
cholera broke out in a very severe form, and the
camp was moved about between November 20 and
December 5, when the disease finally disappeared.
The casualties in the troop were two gunners, four
matrosses, and three lascars.

The troop mustered October 1 at camp Golanti
on the Trunk Road; November 1, camp Salana; and
December 1 at camp Eride. It mustered at camp
Uchár January 1, at Lanuchi February 1, two places
on the Sind River not far apart, on March 1 at
Itmadpur, near Agra, and it arrived at Meerut on the
15th of that month.

1818. This year saw the abolition of the term Fire-
worker and Captain-Lieutenant; the latter became
first lieutenant and the former second lieutenant
(G.G.O. October 17), gunners became bombardiers,
and matrosses, gunners (G.G.O. September 1).

1820. In January 1820 the troop marched for
Mhow, arriving there the next month.

1821. In this year Captain Boileau, having been promoted major, was succeeded by Captain Thomas Lumsden, an officer of considerable merit. Two of his sons, though they did not wear blue, attained high rank in the Bengal Army—Colonel H. B. Lumsden, commanding the Guides in 1857, and the present Sir Peter Lumsden, G.C.B. At the end of 1821 the troop moved again to Meerut.

1824. The war with Burmah had now commenced. The 1st troop was again selected for this service. It left Meerut in July, the guns being sent by water down the Ganges. After remaining at Cawnpore from July to October, the troop proceeded, and by the end of the year was in camp at Ballygunj, near Calcutta.

1825. February 1 saw the troop in camp at Rangoon. It moved up by land with the Commander-in-Chief's column beyond Tharawah, at the head of the delta, but the force had to return as far as Donabyo, where General Cotton's attack had failed. A second attempt on April 1 was successful. Sir A. Campbell mentioned the energy and activity of the Bengal Horse Artillery and Rocket troop under Captains Lumsden and Graham. The army advanced to Prome, where Lieutenant A. Thompson died, May 11. Here the troop remained till December. Prome was blockaded by the enemy, and on the 1st of that month Sir A. Campbell commenced the attack, repeated again at Napadion on December 2.

Captain Lumsden was nearly killed by the explosion of a shell, withdrawn from a howitzer that had twice missed fire. He was thrown down, severely scorched and contused, but sprang up and continued to direct the fire of his gun, not even returning himself in the list of wounded. For this he was mentioned in Sir A. Campbell's despatch. The blockade was completely broken up. One lascar killed and eleven gunners wounded in the 1st troop were the artillery casualties this day.

The troop had now, by the reorganisation in G.G.O. June 24, which added five more troops, become the 1st troop 1st Brigade, R.H.A.

1826. The army continued to advance, and on January 1, 1826, was at Patanajo. The Burmese were making another stand at Malloon, on the right bank of the Irawádi. Batteries were constructed on the night of the 18th and next day opened fire. Lieutenant Henry Havelock, the D.A.A.G., afterwards of Lucknow fame, wrote thus :

'It was evident that the artillerists had hit the range at once. Balls were seen to strike the works . . . demolishing the defences and ploughing up the area of the square. Shells hit sometimes a few paces from the parapet, behind which the garrison was crouching, bursting among their ranks ; sometimes upon the huts of the troops and marked points of the pagodas. The rockets flew in the truest path . . . twice the line of the barbarians . . . gave way

c

under the dreadful fire; twice they were rallied by
their chiefs.' Captain Lumsden was again honourably mentioned by Sir A. Campbell.

Further advance and more fighting took place,
till on February 23 the Burmese King gave in.
Captain Lumsden was one of the officers de-
puted to Ava with some formal presents for the
King.

The troop left Nandabo early in March, and
Captain Lumsden reached Dum Dum with his
head-quarters in the end of April. Lieutenant Grant
was with a detail with Brigadier Blair, and rejoined
at Dum Dum, June 10. Lieutenant G. T. Graham
was with Brigadier Stewart with another detail, and
rejoined June 25. The troop remained there till the
end of the year.

1827. The troop, having left Dum Dum on or
about December 1, 1826, marched by the Grand
Trunk Road and reached Cawnpore on February 14.
It did not remain long there, being sent on to Saugar,
where it arrived by October.

1828-29. It was back at Cawnpore about June
1828, and next year, after practice, marched to Muttra, where it arrived February 27.

1832. In 1832 Captain Lumsden was appointed
Agent for Gun Carriages at Fatehgarh, and was succeeded by Captain Thomas Nicholl. This officer had
served with the 4th troop 3rd Brigade for thirteen
years and had only been posted on his promotion,

four months before, to the 2nd company 3rd Battalion, so that, with the exception of the first two years of his life in the army, his service, to the day of his death ten years afterwards, was continuously with the Horse Artillery.

1837. The troop this year marched to Meerut, from Meerut to Karnal. Captain Lumsden had in acknowledgment of his services been retained on the rolls of the troop; he became a major in the Brevet of January 17 and on his promotion regimentally was struck off.

1840. The troop was under orders for Afghanistan to relieve Captain Grant's troop, which was returning to India. A Mountain Train Battery, H.M. 44th Regiment, and two regiments of Native cavalry were collected at Karnal.

On October 20, the troop, with one of the cavalry regiments and the head-quarters of the 44th Regiment, marched. (The night before, a terrific storm of thunder, lightning, and hail fell; so heavy that in the morning the bungalows were surrounded with a frozen heap.) The rest followed next day. The leading column was at:

	Camp			
Bukrala	.	.	.	December 5
Jani ki Sung	.	.	.	December 13
Jellalabad	.	.	.	April 25

1841. There were some operations in the Nazian Valley, but not very important ones. Captain Nicholl had only two subalterns with him, Waller and C. Stewart.

The cantonment formed at Kabul was an oblong parallelogram, commanded from without, and in every respect unfitted for defence. The Commissariat stores in a detached fort about 200 yards towards the city.

On November 2, Sir Alexander Burnes' quarters in the city were attacked, and he, his brother, and Lieutenant Broadfoot, were murdered.

This was the beginning of the outbreak which ended in the destruction of the whole force. Captain Nicholl and Lieutenant Stewart were sent into the Bala Hissar Fort, where the whole force should have been stationed, if it were not to have retired on Jellalabad, before the tribes had risen.

On November 3, Lieutenant Waller's guns supported a sortie under Major Swayne in clearing out the gardens between cantonments, where they rendered efficient aid, and Waller was severely wounded ; Lieutenant Vincent Eyre then took command of his guns.

Every day had its share of fighting. On November 9 one of the Horse Artillery guns and one Mountain Train gun were sent from the Bala Hissar and reached cantonments.

On the 10th a force was sent out and secured the Rika Bashi Fort. Lieutenant Eyre, with two guns of the troop and one of the Mountain Train, rendered

SERGEANT MULHALL AND HIS DETACHMENT

Cutting their way through the enemy at the action of Beh Maree outside Kabul 13th November, 1842.

the most essential service, driving off the enemy at close quarters with grape.

On the 13th an attack was made on the enemy, who had occupied the Beh Maree heights; Lieutenant Eyre, with one troop and one Mountain Train gun, accompanied. Twice they were driven back up the hill, leaving their two guns. As the ground there was impracticable for Horse Artillery, Lieutenant Eyre took forward a gunner with drag-ropes and spikes; one, a 4-pounder, was removed by the infantry, the other, a 6-pounder, was under a heavy fire, so Eyre and the gunner got down to it and spiked it. The 4-pounder was brought in.

Another attack was made on the Beh Maree position on the 22nd, but it was fruitless. Lieutenant Eyre received a shot through the left hand, and was for a time incapacitated. Next day another attack was made on the same position, but it was still more disastrous. One gun under Sergeant Mulhall was sent, the Mountain Train gun having been disabled, and Major-General Elphinstone anxious to retain the other gunners in cantonments. The force reached the top of the hill before daylight, but soon were surrounded, and the 5th Native Infantry became disheartened. The single gun maintained an effective fire, but it had no support, and the vent ere long got too hot to be served and they were cut off, the rest having fled.

'Here, amidst so much that was condemnable, let me again bear just and heartfelt testimony to the behaviour of that brave though small body of men, whose conduct on this and on every other occasion during the war was that of a band of heroes, and who, preferring death to dishonour, met their fate, nobly fighting for the gun they had so ably served; I allude to the Horse Artillery, when Sergeant Mulhall and six gunners whose names I feel deep sorrow I cannot here record, sword in hand, awaited the advance of the foe, and it was not until they saw themselves alone, in the midst of thousands of the enemy, that they dashed at full gallop, cutting their way through them down the hill, and, though surrounded by cavalry and infantry, yet they managed to bring their gun safely to the plain, where, however, only three of them being alive, and they desperately wounded, they were obliged to leave it and contrived to reach cantonments. . . . So gallant did Sir W. Macnaughten consider the behaviour of this sergeant, that he promised to bring the same to the notice of Government.' (Narrative of Captain Johnson.)   Lieutenant Eyre in his narrative says : 'Sergeant Mulhall escaped by a miracle, his clothes perforated with bullets.' A second limber was sent out and reached them, so there may have been a sergeant and twelve men engaged. Captain Johnson gives the casualties this day at four killed and six wounded. This action decided the fate of the force. Negotiations for a retreat were entered into at the second interview with Akbar Khan. The envoy, Sir

CAPTAIN THOMAS NICHOLL.

Killed in action when in command of the Troop during the retreat
from Kabul.

W. Macnaughten, was murdered. Major Eldred Pottinger unwillingly consented to Akbar Khan's terms. Hostages were given up, and all guns save six.

1842. On January 6 the army commenced its retreat; on the 7th the Mountain Train guns were lost; the ladies and children were given up. Assistant-Surgeon Alexander Bryce, of the Horse Artillery, was killed at Tazmi on the 9th. Jagdallak was reached on the afternoon of the 11th. Captain Nicholl, with his surviving men acting as dragoons, charged and routed a body of the enemy. But few reached Gandamuk on the 13th. Where Captain Nicholl and Lieutenant Greene fell is not known, but the 13th is the official date of their death and of Charles Stewart, last of the artillery to end his soldier's career.

The survivors of the troop were:

Lieutenant R. Waller, wife and two children.

Sergeant Malcolm McNee.

Sergeant M. F. Cleland.

Gunner A. Hearne.

Gunner Keen.

Gunner Dalton.

All prisoners in Akbar Khan's hands, given up as hostages or wounded.

Gunner Swindell and Gunner Charles Deane were laboratory men at Jellalabad.

As soon as the news of these disasters reached India, orders were given for the formation of a troop

to replace this one.   G.O. February 16 directed the
2nd troop 2nd Brigade, the 1st, 2nd, and 3rd of the
3rd Brigade to furnish each three N.C.O.s and thirteen gunners, and five companies six gunners each ;
Brevet Major W. Geddes to command.   This was
done at Meerut.

1843.   Next year, Major Geddes having been promoted, Captain Francis Dashwood was appointed.

1844.   In 1844 the troop moved to Loodiana.

1845.   Next year it suffered a good deal from
fever, and so, when Sir Henry Hardinge was moving
up troops to meet the Sikhs on the Sutlej, it was
not contemplated to employ it on service.   But
on December 13 the Governor-General, Prince
Waldemar of Prussia, with Counts Gröben and
Oriola, were dining at the troop mess ; and so, when
at eight o'clock Captain O'Hanlon brought the
wished-for order that the troop was to march the
following morning, Captain Dashwood and his sub-
altern, Lieutenant Tombs, got on a pony and rode
down to the barracks with the good news.   Only
four guns, however, were sent.   On the 18th the
battle of Mudki was fought.   The Sikh line was
supported by a strong artillery.   Their fire in the
centre was very severe.   The troop, with two guns
of the Governor-General's escort under Lieutenant
Moir attached to it (these two guns belonged to the
2/3 H.A., now 57th R.F.A.), advanced with the rest
of the artillery, forty-two guns in all, and engaged the

centre of the Sikh army until the arrival of the infantry, when the troop, with 1/3 H.A. (now 'L' Battery) and 4/3 H.A., moved with Brigadier Mactier's brigade of cavalry to the left, and attacked the enemy's right flank. Later, when the infantry attack on the centre was checked, the troop was brought up to support the attack at this point. Here the fighting was most severe. Captain Dashwood received severe wounds by grape-shot in the arm and foot, from which he died on the following day. The fight continued till darkness put an end to the conflict; the enemy slowly retired before our advance and finally retreated on Ferozshah. The artillery bivouacked by their guns. The casualties in the six troops of Horse Artillery in this battle were seventy-four of all ranks killed and wounded and fifty-four horses.

The army moved forward, and on the 21st was commenced the battle of Ferozshah. Captain L. E. Mills was temporarily in command of the troop. It was in the centre of the two wings, commanded by the Commander-in-Chief and the Governor-General, Moir's two guns on its left. All the batteries, horse and foot, in advance of the line of infantry, kept up a hot fire on the entrenchments, and finally got within, but were withdrawn by Brigadier Brooke on account of the danger to the ammunition from powder buried or loosely scattered about. Brigadier Brooke, in fact, reported

one, perhaps a second waggon, exploded in the troop
and both of Lieutenant Moir's. When it was quite
dark the troops were withdrawn, as the entrenchments were still partly held by the Sikhs. Sir Harry
Smith, with part of his division, occupied the village
in the centre. The two chiefs bivouacked about
two hundred yards south-west of the entrenchments.
Besides the troop and Moir's guns, the 4th troop
3rd Brigade were here; D'Arcy Todd's troop not far
off; General Littler's division some distance off, on
the road to Ferozepore, and the rest further behind;
head-quarters at Misriwala. The Sikhs kept up
a galling fire during the early part of the night, and
more than once the troop had to turn out.

Next morning the separated portions of the
army united and swept through the entrenchments,
driving out the remaining Sikhs. But they were
still in large numbers on the further side, and, though
the ammunition boxes had been refilled from the
spare waggons, there was not much left. Suddenly
Sirdar Tej Singh appeared with a large and fresh
body of the enemy. A heavy fire was kept up, to
which our guns replied. The troop was now on the
extreme right of our line. After a time the enemy
appeared to be moving away to their left; our guns
were silent by 2 P.M. No fresh attack came; then
our artillery got the extraordinary order to proceed
to Ferozepore from Army Head-quarters, but without
the knowledge of Sir Hugh Gough, Lord Hardinge, or

Brigadier Brooke, commanding the artillery. However, no harm came of it, and by 10 the next morning they were back at Ferozshah. Tej Singh was accused, not without strong grounds, of having acted the traitor.

1846. Captain C. E. Mills had reverted to his position on the Governor-General's Staff and Lieutenant J. Mills was in command of the troop. Sir Harry Smith had been sent to Loodiana, as Ranja Singh had crossed the Sutlej and was supposed to be about to attack that station. Brigadier C. Cureton, with his cavalry and the troop, were sent after him, joining Smith, January 26. Ranja Singh was then at Aliwal. Sir Harry Smith marched there on the 28th and attacked. The ground was open, the day fine, the dispositions good, and the advance was described as performed with the accuracy of a well-ordered field day — four infantry brigades in the centre, cavalry on the flanks, two troops in each of the intervals between the infantry brigades of Hicks and Wheeler, a field battery between Hicks and Godby ; but as they advanced, the guns, as usual going to the front, acted in unison against the enemy's line. The 1st troop was on the right of the Horse Artillery guns, the field battery on its outer flank. 'Our guns,' said Sir H. Smith, ' being constantly ahead of everything . . . our guns and gunners, officers and men, may be equalled, but not excelled by any artillery in the world.'

Such praise from an old Peninsular officer is no slight commendation. Mr. McAuliffe, Riding-Master, 2nd Brigade H.A., who had served in the 1st troop almost from the first, acted as a Staff officer to Major G. E. Laurenson, and was mentioned by him in his despatch. Lieutenant H. Tombs also acted on Sir Harry Smith's Staff as A.D.C., and was likewise mentioned with praise.

The troop did not rejoin the army, but was transferred to Brigadier Wheeler's force, operating against Fort Kangan. It was in charge of the heavy train. After this it returned to Loodiana. Captain R. H. Baldwin, just promoted, was retransferred from the 4th troop to command.

1848. The troop was not actively employed in the second Sikh war, but was sent to Ferozepore in the latter part of November.

1849. When the army of the Punjab was broken up, G.O. March 23, 1849, ordered the troop, on relief by the 3rd troop 2nd Brigade, to Jullundur. The latter went to Jullundur in the end of November and the 1st troop proceeded to Wazirabad; when
1850.   the cantonments at Sialkot were ready, it shifted into them.

1851. From Sialkot the troop marched to Peshawar. The tribes on the frontier, always a lawless lot, gave us for many years a good deal of trouble.

1852.   Sir Colin Campbell, commanding at

Peshawar, was out again, this time to punish the Swát people of the Ranizai tribe. The 1st troop went with the force, a large one, in March. The Ranizai Maliks submitted, but, having refused to pay the fine imposed, a larger force was taken on May 15. The chief of Tanji was attacked, and his villages destroyed. Thence Sir Colin went to Skákot, where the Swátis had collected; they were dispersed with heavy loss, and the villages and crops destroyed on May 18. The ground was broken, and intersected by a steep wide nullah which the gunners held well. Major Baldwin and both his subalterns were among those that were thanked, and the General mentioned more particularly the artillery under Major Baldwin, to whom he was indebted for the comparatively small loss incurred on our side. The India medal was awarded for this service.

1854. In this year the troop moved to Meerut, where it remained till the beginning of 1857. Major Baldwin, having gone home with the intention of retiring, Major H. A. Olpherts was appointed to command from the 3rd company 6th Battalion and No. 19 Field Battery.

1857. The troop marched from Meerut, February 6, for Jullundur. On May 10 the sepoy outbreak began at Meerut; at Jullundur on June 7. Major Olpherts had his guns out; but the brigadier would not let him act. The native troop, the 5th of the 1st Brigade (now T. battery R.H.A.), arrived that

morning, and did act, without orders, except from
their own officers. The Native cavalry coming down
on them, to get them to join them, were sent to the
right-about with grape. Lieutenant Dobbin had
been sent with two guns to Phillour to protect
the magazine. On June 23, Major Olpherts, with
four guns, and two of the 5th troop, arrived at
Delhi, fifteen days after the siege had commenced.

Lieutenants Lindsay and Cumberland came with
him, Lieutenant Dobbin being left at Phillour to
assist in the magazine. Lieutenant Traill arrived
with the remaining section on the 28th. From this
time till the capture of Delhi the troop was daily
engaged. Major Olpherts, whose health had for some
time not been good, was on the sick list early in
August, and Captain Rimmington was temporarily
placed in command. On August 12 a force under
Brigadier G. D. Showers attacked the rebels, who,
about the Khudsia Bagh, were annoying us at the
Metcalf picquet. The troop was employed. The
enemy were completely surprised and four guns taken.

On the 25th, Brigadier-General Nicholson was
sent with a force to follow a large body of the
rebels, known to have gone out to intercept the
siege train coming down from Phillour. The troop
was again sent out with the other Horse Artillery
guns. The rebels were attacked at Najafgarh
and driven back to Delhi, losing thirteen guns.

For the day of assault, September 14, the left

half troop was to have accompanied No. 4 Column under Major Reid, directed against Kissengung, but, as most of the men were with Major Rimmington in the breaching batteries, it could not be used, as they could not be relieved in time, and there were only enough men, besides, to man one gun. The right half troop was with the cavalry under Brigadier Hope Grant, and it rendered essential service against the Mori Bastion and the Cabul Gate. The Burn Bastion and the Telewara suburb plied the attack with grape. Every building was full of rebels. Lieutenant Lindsay was again wounded (the other occasion being at Najafgarh), but slightly; a gunner, a lascar, and four horses were killed and nine horses wounded. Lieutenant Traill spiked two guns in the Telewara suburb. Lindsay was mentioned in Hope Grant's despatch, Lindsay and Traill in that of Major Gaitskell, commanding the whole of the artillery.

Taking the season, the sickness, and the paucity of our numbers into consideration, the operations against Delhi from June 8 to September 22 were as splendid as any in the annals of the British Army. The troop left Delhi on September 28 with a force, under Brigadier E. H. Greathed, to clear the country between the Ganges and Jumna, and open communications with Cawnpore. The officers present with it were Captain Rimmington and Lieutenants H. Murray, Lindsay, and Manderson. They reached Bulandshahr on the 28th, where Malidan Khan, the local chief, made a stand but was defeated. There were some wounded here. After a halt of four days, the column marched, October 3, to Khurja, on the 5th was at Aligarh, and on the 6th at Akbarabad, where an urgent requisition came from Agra. On the morning of the 10th the force was there, after a very long march. The horses had just been watered and fed, when shot came rolling into the camp. Agra had been asleep, but the men were out at once; gunners in their shirt-sleeves replying to the fire as the horses were being hooked in. The force soon advanced, the troop on the right, and the enemy were driven across the Kheri Nudda, leaving thirteen guns in our hands. The distance covered by the time they returned to camp was sixty-six miles in thirty-nine hours.

On the 14th the column marched for Cawnpore, which it reached on the 26th. Here Sir Colin Campbell was assembling a large force for the relief of Lucknow and second relief of the leaguered Residency. It marched to the Alum Bagh on November 12. The troop now had only five guns, not being able to man more with facility. On the 14th the Residency was reached, after very hard fighting. It was evacuated, by the Chief's order, by the 23rd, and the army marched back to Cawnpore, already attacked by very large forces from the Gwalior side, notice of which was received at Bunni on the 27th. So the chief pushed on.

The troop crossed the river at 8 A.M. and took

up a post with Brigadier Adrian Hope's brigade, near the Cavalry Lines, covering the road to Allahabad; for all the ladies, women and children, &c., from the Residency had to be sent down to Calcutta before anything could be done, and four or five days elapsed before they were all cleared off.

Then the chief attacked. The troop, with Longden's and Blunt's guns, were on the left. The rebels, though largely augmented in numbers by Oudh men, were forced back and chased along the Kalpi Road, leaving behind many of their guns.

Two days after, the troop accompanied Brigadier Hope Grant with a force towards Bithoor. The rebels were attacked at Shivrajpur and dispersed, with loss of all their guns and heavily in men. Grant then returned to Cawnpore. On the 24th the Commander-in-Chief took a large force towards Fatehgurh. The rebels were again caught up, and defeated at Kali Nuddi on January 2. The troop was not engaged here.

1858. In February the troop, under Rimmington, now a brevet major, was sent to reinforce Sir James Outram at the Alum Bagh, south of Lucknow. In March the large army intended for the recapture of Lucknow was assembled. On the 6th Sir James Outram was sent across the Gumti River, to co-operate with the chief on the right of the main attack. The value of this move was by no means subservient to that of the main body. The

D

rebel positions were one by one successively enfiladed, and, had Outram been given a free hand, the force could have accomplished more. He rejoined Sir Colin Campbell on the 14th. While the heavier metal was doing the direct work, the Horse Artillery were actively employed everywhere in co-operating. Major Rimmington's name was recorded for honourable mention. He was now appointed to command the 3rd troop 3rd Brigade, and Brevet Major William Olpherts was ordered to do duty with the troop while his cousin was on furlough. The latter (H. A. Olpherts) was promoted brevet lieutenant-colonel, June 16, but W. Olpherts (now brevet lieutenant-colonel) was appointed Prize Agent, and his place was taken by Brevet Major H. Le G. Bruce from the 4th company 5th Battalion (G.O. June 10).

After the capture of Lucknow the troop remained as part of the large force then under Sir Hope Grant, who had to make or send several expeditions against the rebels, still swarming all over Oudh. The troop was out on one of these to the north in April, at Kussi, again to Jasenda, S.S.E. of Lucknow, in June, after which at Nawabgunj, on the Cawnpore Road in a standing camp, under Brigadier Evelegh. Here Lieutenants W. D. Couchman and C. H. Barnes, whose troop had mutinied at Neemuch, joined, and Lieutenant Dixon was posted. Lieutenants Lindsay and Traill had

F' GUN, MEERUT

INSCRIPTION. 'F' GUN. MEERUT.

gone away sick, and Lieutenant Murray had gone back to his troop after the capture of Lucknow.

In August the troop was employed against rebels at Husaingunj, and again at Miangunj on October 5, returning to the camp at Nawabgunj after each expedition or daur, as they were called. In November the troop was again out against a strong fort called Dhundia Khera. Lieutenants Manderson and Barnes were on this service with four guns.

After this the troop went to Faizabad and then to Gonda.

1859. In February the troop went to Lucknow, and were stationed in the Marino. Lieutenant-Colonel H. A. Olpherts had returned from leave home, and taken over command. The last of the rebel sepoys were being hunted over our frontier into Nípal.

1860. From Lucknow the troop moved to Benares. Lieutenant-Colonel Olpherts had again been obliged to take sick leave to the Hills. He died at Landour on November 11 of abscess of the liver. Had his health permitted, he would have risen to higher distinction, for no one knew his duties better, or was more prompt in fulfilling them. Captain H. P. de Teissier succeeded him in the command ; he had been in the Native company and field battery at Delhi when the mutiny broke out.

1861. The amalgamation of the Indian with the Royal Artillery was now to be carried out. A circular was sent to each officer, and the result was as expected—only four officers of the Bengal Artillery elected for local service.

Regimental Order, May 21, 1861, published the following telegram from the Commander-in-Chief, Sir Hugh Rose, to the commandant of artillery :

' I congratulate you and the officers, non-commissioned officers, and men of your noble corps on the fine military feeling which has prompted them to volunteer almost universally to serve the Queen anywhere.'

And G.G.O., October 14, with G.O. Queen's troops, October 28, transferred the 1st troop 1st Brigade Bengal Horse Artillery under the designation of ' A ' Battery 2nd Royal Horse Brigade.

The above was transcribed from the manuscript of Major-General F. W. Stubbs, late Bengal Artillery, author of ' The History of the Bengal Artillery.'

The battery remained at Benares till 1863, when it marched to Morar, Gwalior, whence in 1864 it moved to Calcutta, whence it embarked on **1865.** January 14, 1865, under the command of Captain J. R. Sladen, for England, and disembarked at Woolwich on April 26. The battery served in England till 1873, being quartered at the following stations :

1866. Aldershot.

1867. Dorchester.

1869. Aldershot.

1871. Woolwich.

1873. On January 16, 1873, the battery embarked for India, under command of Major M. M. FitzGerald, on board H.M.S. ' Serapis,' and arrived at Meerut on March 5.

1874. The battery attended the Delhi Durbar in March and April, and was on escort duty with H.R.H. the Prince of Wales during his visit to India at Delhi and Agra in December 1875 and January and February 1876, and was present at the Imperial Assemblage, at Delhi, when Her Majesty Queen Victoria was proclaimed Empress of India on **1877.** January 1, 1877. From Delhi the battery marched to Mian Mir, and was quartered there till the outbreak of the war with Afghanistan in **1878.** October 1878. This year the designation of the battery was changed, and it became ' A ' Battery, ' B ' Brigade, R.H.A.

In October 1878 the battery marched to Mooltan, under command of Brevet-Colonel McFarlan, and joined the cavalry brigade, under Lieut.-General Sir Donald Stewart, commanding the 1st Division of the Kandahar Field Force. The constitution of this force was as follows :

15th Hussars, 8th and 19th Bengal Cavalry ; A/B, R.H.A. ; I/1, D/1, G/4, R.F.A. ; 13/8, 16/8, 5/11, 6/11, 8/11, and 11/11, R.G.A.

Two companies of Sappers and Miners, 2/60 Rifles, 59th Foot, 15th and 23rd Bengal Infantry, and 1st and 3rd Gurkhas.

After a short halt at Jacobabad, the force marched on December 1 through the Dadar and Bolan Passes to Quetta, suffering great loss in baggage animals through dearth of supplies. From Quetta they marched to the Khoja Amran Range, where they joined the 2nd Division under General Michael Biddulph, and crossed the Khojak Pass on December 30.

1879. On January 2, 1879, the advance to Kandahar commenced, on the two roads leading from the Khojak and Ghwaja Passes. On January 4, when crossing the Mel Valley, the cavalry brigade came in contact with the enemy's cavalry, and drove them through the Ghlo Pass. The battery came into action on the further side, doing considerable execution. Captain R. G. S. Marshall and Lieutenant J. F. P. Hamilton were mentioned in General Palliser's despatches for their conduct in this action. The enemy fled towards Kandahar, which was occupied without further opposition on January 8.

On January 15 the battery left with the 1st Division for Khelat-i-Ghilzie, ninety miles on the Ghuzni Road. The fort was found evacuated, and the force remained there on short rations from January 21 to February 6, the mortality amongst the horses and camels being very great through want of food and inadequate covering. The battery lost twenty horses on this expedition. On February 6 the force commenced its return march to Kandahar, which was reached on Febuary 28.

On June 1 the battery moved into huts, and on July 19 into cholera camp. At this time it suffered severely from cholera, no fewer than fifteen men succumbing to that disease between July 14 and August 3.

On May 26 a treaty of peace had been signed at Gandamuk, and Northern Afghanistan had been evacuated by the middle of June, but the retirement from Kanhahar had been postponed until the autumn for sanitary reasons.

On August 4 the battery moved with other troops into the Peshin Valley, where it remained until, on the news of the murder of the British Envoy at Kabul on September 3, the troops were concentrated at Kandahar, where (with the exception of General Hughes's operations at Khelat-i-Ghilzie, in which the battery did not take part) nothing of importance occurred during the invasion of Northern Afghanistan and occupation of Kabul by General Roberts.

1880. Towards the end of January 1880 it was decided that, in view of renewed operations in the spring, the Bengal troops under Sir Donald Stewart's command should be held in readiness to move from Kandahar on Ghuzni and open up communication with Kabul.

On the arrival of the relieving troops from India

the advance commenced, and the Ghazni Field Force
marched from Kandahar for Kabul on March 30.

The force was constituted as follows :

CAVALRY BRIGADE.

A/B, R.H.A., 19th B.L., 6/11 R.A., 19th P.I.
and Div. Hd. Qrs.

1ST INFANTRY BRIGADE.

1st P.C., 11/11 R.A., 2/60 Rifles, 15th Sikhs,
and 25th P.I.

2ND INFANTRY BRIGADE.

2nd P.C., G/4 R.A., 59th Foot, 3rd Gurkhas,
2nd Sikhs.

Khelat-i-Ghilzie was reached on April 6, and
until Shah-Jin was passed supplies were plentiful,
but beyond that great difficulties were experienced,
the inhabitants having deserted their villages and
destroyed or buried their grain.   No active opposition
was met with till Ghazni was neared, though a
hostile gathering had been observed marching some
eight miles to the right of the columns.

On April 18, the force encamped at Mushaki, and
at dawn on the following day the cavalry brigade
and divisional head-quarters moved off, followed by
the 2nd Brigade, then the baggage, and lastly the
1st Brigade as rear guard, the column being some

six miles long. About an hour after leaving camp the enemy were reported in great strength on a range of hills crossing the Ghazni Road three miles to the front, near the village of Ahmed Khel. A/B, with the cavalry, moved to the front and took up a position on a knoll about 1,500 yards from the enemy. No sooner had they done so than dense swarms of the enemy, both horse and foot, came rolling down on to the head of the column. For a short time the battery had alone to stem the rush, then G/4, R.A., galloped into action on their left, and the fire of the two batteries carried destruction into the advancing hordes, who soon advanced to case-shot range. All the case-shot was expended, and resort was had to inverted shrapnel. The order was now given for the guns to retire, as there was a considerable gap between them and the infantry on their left rear; and they fell back steadily to a knoll some 120 yards in rear covered by charges of the 2nd Punjab Cavalry. So near were the Ghazies when the last gun was limbered up that a gunner was nearly cut down as he mounted. Meanwhile other hordes of the enemy had swept down on the left, where the 60th Rifles, 59th Foot, 2nd Sikhs, 3rd Gurkhas, and 10th Punjab Infantry faced them on a line parallel to the line of advance; and on the left rear, where gallant charges of the 19th Bengal Cavalry failed to check them, and for a short time all in that part of the field was in confusion; even the Head-quarter

Staff having to prepare to defend themselves with swords drawn. But the steady fire of the 3rd Gurkhas, who had been forced to form rallying squares, and the fire of 6/11 Heavy battery from a knoll further to the left, soon restored the battle, and the enemy's swarms recoiled from all sides like a wave which has spent its force against a rocky shore. They broke and fled to their hills, leaving over a thousand of their number dead and dying on the ground. General Barter, with the 1st Brigade, arrived towards the close of the action, and the cease fire was sounded at 10 A.M. The casualties of the British force amounted to seventeen killed and one hundred and twenty-four wounded, among whom was Captain R. Corbett, of the battery. After halting two hours, the force moved forward across the enemy's position and completed a seventeen-mile march to Nani.

Major May, in his 'Achievements of Field Artillery,' in commenting on this action, says : 'Nevertheless, it is strictly true to say that the honours of the day rested with the guns, and that, had they not stemmed the first rush as they did, almost alone, our losses, even supposing no worse result had ensued, would have been immensely heavier. As it was, it is not too much to say that no artillery has ever been called upon to repel a more determined charge upon them, a charge which no Europeans would probably ever have ventured to make at all, and which they certainly would

'A' BATTERY 'B' BRIGADE, R.H.A. IN ACTION AT AHMED KHEL.

never have made with the same ferocity and reck-
lessness.'

On the following day the advanced cavalry reached
Ghuzni, and the force halted there for three days,
communication being opened up with General
Ross's column, which had been sent out from Kabul
for that purpose. Here in the fort of Ghuzni were
found two of the guns lost by the battery in the
disastrous retreat from Kabul in 1842. These guns
were taken back to India by the battery. One is
now at Meerut, and the other was presented to the
battery by the Indian Government on September 20,
1899.

On April 22, a force consisting of A/B, R.H.A. ;
11/11 R.A. ; 2/60 Rifles, 15th Sikhs, 25th P.I., and
2nd Sikhs, and 1st and 2nd P.C., under General
Palliser, moved out to dislodge a force of the enemy
reported to be occupying a position about six miles
south-east of the camp, which was found too strong
to attack. Reinforcements were heliographed for,
and Sir Donald Stewart soon arrived with the 59th
Foot, 3rd Gurkhas, a half battalion 19 P.I., the
15th B.L., and G/4 R.A. General Stewart at once
formed for the attack. The R.H.A., the cavalry,
and 1st infantry brigade on the right, were to attack
the village of Shatez, and the remainder of the troops
on the left to assault Arzu village. The attack commenced, A/B effectively shelling both villages, and
by 12.30 all was over. The enemy fled, pursued by

the cavalry and Horse Artillery, one half battery on the right, under Lieutenant Hamilton, and the other on the left, under Major Carter, galloping forward to within 800 yards of the enemy and doing great execution : 411 rounds were fired this day. The loss of the enemy was about 400.

On April 27 a junction was effected at Doaba, about forty miles north of Ghuzni, with the column under General Ross, which had had some severe fighting on their march from Kabul. From Doaba the Ghuzni Field Force moved to the right into the Logar Valley and became the 3rd Division Northern Afghanistan Field Force, under Major-General Hills, C.B., V.C. At the latter end of June the force moved from Hissarak to Charasiab, and thence on the 30th of that month to Zargunshahr, twenty-five miles from Kabul, where a successful cavalry action was fought against the Zermuttis at Putkao Shana. At the end of July the battery marched to Kabul, and encamped on the Siah Sung Heights east of the city on August 4. On July 22 Abdul Rahman was proclaimed Amir of Afghanistan, and on the 27th of that month occurred the disastrous battle of Maiwand, in which Ayub Khan, who was advancing from Herat on Kandahar, defeated the British force under General Burrowes, and Kandahar was besieged.

On the receipt of the news of these events at Kabul it was determined that they should not interfere with the evacuation of Northern Afghanistan, and that while the force under General Roberts

moved to the relief of Kandahar the remainder of
the troops should retire to India. So, on August
17, the battery left Kabul and marched, *via* the
Khyber Pass, to India, arriving at Fort Jamrud on
August 26, having been one year and nine months
across the frontier. Its losses during that period
had been thirty-two N.C.O.s and men and thirty-five
horses. Major Warter (commanding) and Captain
R. Corbett were both granted brevet rank for their
services.

The battery arrived at Umballa on December 2,
and was stationed there until it proceeded home to
England in H.M.S. 'Serapis' in January 1882.

It served at home till September 1895, being
quartered at the following stations :

1882. Dorchester.

1885. Dublin.

1889. Woolwich.

1893. Aldershot.

1895. Woolwich.

In 1888 the battery was rearmed with the 12-
pounder equipment, and on September 1, 1889, its
designation was changed to 'F' Battery, R.H.A.

On January 20, 1892, a gun-carriage and detachment, under Lieutenant White Thomson,
was sent to Sandringham to attend the funeral of
H.R.H. the Duke of Clarence, on which occasion
H.R.H. the Prince of Wales officially notified
his satisfaction at the admirable turn-out of the
detachment.

While quartered at Aldershot the battery greatly distinguished itself in the football field, winning the Artillery challenge shield two years in succession ; it also won the R.H.A. driving competition at the Royal Military Tournament in 1894.

On September 17, 1895, the battery, under command of Major F. L. Cunliffe, embarked in the hired transport 'Britannia' for India, and was stationed at Sialkot, relieving 'Q' Battery, R.H.A.·

During the spring and summer of 1897 a spirit of unrest pervaded the tribes on the North-West Frontier, whose fanaticism was aroused by the preaching of their mullahs, by a book lately published by the Amir of Afghanistan on the subject of Jehad, or the Holy War, and by the successes of the Turks in their war with Greece.

Disturbances broke out in the Tochi Valley, into which an expedition was sent, and in July the Malakand was furiously attacked by tribes from the Swat Valley. Reinforcements were hurried up to the threatened points, and on August 13 the battery and the 11th (P.A.O.) Hussars were ordered to proceed on relief scale to Rawul Pindi to relieve ' K ' Battery and the 4th Dragoon Guards, which had been sent to garrison Fort Jamrud, at the entrance to the Khyber Pass. The order was received at 8 A.M., and the battery entrained the same afternoon and proceeded, under command of Lieutenant Harman, to Rawul Pindi. After the action of Shubkhudar, in which the Mohmunds who had raided the Peshawar Valley north of the Kabul River were defeated, reinforcements were urgently required at Peshawar, and at 9 A.M. on August 18 orders were received for the battery and two squadrons of the 11th Hussars to proceed at once on field service scale to Peshawar. In a few hours the battery was mobilised, and with ' A ' and ' C ' squadrons 11th Hussars was entrained by 5 o'clock in the afternoon and arrived at Peshawar at 3 o'clock A.M. on the 19th and occupied the lines of the 51st Battery, R.F.A., which had been moved out to Shubkhudar.

On August 23 the Afridis rose, and attacked and captured Lundi Kotal and other posts in the Khyber. ' K,' R.H.A., was in action against them, and by their fire drove them from Fort Maude, near the entrance to the Pass, and enabled the garrison of Khyber Rifles to escape. On the evening of the 24th the battery was ordered out with the reserve brigade, as reports were received that the Afridis were going to attack Jamrud that night. It bivouacked at the junction of the Jamrud Road with the Circular Road, to be ready to start at dawn, but nothing more than sniping took place, and the battery took up its quarters in the empty lines of the 52nd O.L.I. close by. On the 29th, all being quiet in the Khyber, it returned to the R.A. lines.

On September 2 news was received that the Mohmunds had collected again, and were advancing

from their valley, so the battery and the 11th Hussars were ordered out at 4 P.M. to reinforce the
troops at Shubkhrdar. The brigade marched fifteen
miles to Adizai, on the northern bank of the Kabul
River. The crossing of the river by the temporary
bridge of boats was an arduous business, the guns
and other carriages having all to be man-handled
across, and they were not all over till 10.30. That
night the Mohmunds retired to their hills, and, as
the Afridis were again active in the Khyber, the
brigade was ordered back to Peshawar on the
following afternoon, and moved out on the morning
of the 4th to Fort Hari Singh, about half-way
between Peshawar and Fort Jamrud, from which
place both the force at Jamrud and that at Fort
Bara, about six miles to the south, could be readily
supported. A wing of a Gurkha regiment occupied
the fort, and the brigade cut down the crops and
pitched their camp on the wet irrigated ground
outside. Entrenchments were thrown up and wire
entanglements laid down round the camp and in
front of the picquets. Here the brigade remained
during the expedition against the Mohmunds under
Brigadier-General Wodehouse and the advance into
and occupation of the Tirah Valley by Sir William
Lockhart. No fighting occurred, but the camp was
occasionally sniped into, and on October 27 a body
of budmashes crept between the picquets through
the crops, which the civil authorities would not

allow to be cut, at about 3 A.M., and rushed the picquets from the rear, killed and wounded several men and carried off their rifles.

The brigade suffered severely from enteric and malarial fever caused by bad water, the foulness of the ground on which the camp was pitched, and the plague of flies. Scarcely an officer or man escaped sickness, and when Sir George Wolseley came out to inspect the post on November 15 only the guns and four men per detachment could be turned out, and the two squadrons of the 11th Hussars were in no better case. Sir George immediately ordered the return of the brigade to Peshawar, which was carried out on the following day. One officer, Lieutenant R. St. C. Harman, and six N.C.O.s and men had died and twelve others were eventually invalided home from disease contracted on this service.

The brigade remained at Peshawar till the end of December, when it returned to Sialkot, arriving there by train on the 29th.

The battery remained at Sialkot until January 1901, when it moved to Rawul Pindi, exchanging stations with 'K' Battery, R.H.A.

1901. This year, on December 24, Sergeant-Major C. Anscomb died. He had served in the battery for thirty-one years, and was present at the battle of Ahmed Khel.

1902. The battery took part in the Euzafzai manœuvres, January 1902, being attached to the

E

cavalry brigade of the Northern Army operating from Nowshera.

1903. The following year it obtained a first class and the badge at the annual practice camp at Hutti, and took part in the Rawul Pindi manœuvres in December of that year, being brigaded with the 3rd Hussars as part of the cavalry division of the Southern Force.

This year the battery was brigaded with 'J' Battery, R.H.A., forming with it the IX Brigade, R.H.A.

The two batteries met at Rawul Pindi in November 1903 on the arrival of 'J' Battery from Meerut. They attended the practice camp at Hutti together, and after that and the manœuvres 'J' Battery relieved 'F' at Rawul Pindi, and 'F' marched to Sialkot, coming there on the war establishment.

APPENDIX

A.

Marches of Lord Lake from Sikandra, in pursuit of Holkar, 1804.

							Miles.
Oct.	1	Chandghur	.	.	.	.	10
,,	2	Shandipur	.	.	.	.	9
,,	3	Near Muttra	.	.	.	.	11 [1]
,,	12	Sait	.	.	.	.	12
,,	13	Chátah	.	.	.	.	13
,,	14	Hodel	.	.	.	.	15
,,	15	Bahminikhera	.	.	.	.	12
,,	16	Sikri	.	.	.	.	17
,,	17	Faridabad	.	.	.	.	11
,,	18	Delhi	.	.	.	.	14 [2]
,,	31	Loni	.	.	.	.	9
Nov.	1	Baghput	.	.	.	.	15
,,	2	Kandlah	.	.	.	.	28
,,	3	Shambi	.	.	.	.	12 [3]
,,	5	Mukamadabad	.	.	.	.	14
,,	6	Hindan Nullah	.	.	.	.	13
,,	7	Khalaoli	.	.	.	.	13

[1] Halted eight days.   [2] Relieved city. Halted twelve days.
     [3] Relieved garrison. Halted one day.

Miles

Nov.	8	Meerut	19
,,	9	Hápar	19
,,	10	Malagkar	19
,,	11	Shikarpur	19
,,	12	Pilaona	19
,,	13	Kauriganj	19
,,	14	Kharganj	20
,,	15	Sherpur	21
,,	16	Aliganj	23
,,	17	Fatehgarh	31 [1]
,,	20	Tiriah	7
,,	21	Bewan	17
,,	22	Mainpuri	17
,,	23	Tsárah	16
,,	24	Etah	19
,,	25	Purah	17
,,	26	Medhu	21
,,	27	Isár	13
,,	28	Satneh	20 [2]
Dec.	1	Aring	6 [3]
,,	3	Keraswámi	9 [4]
,,	11	Kasba	5
,,	12	Deeg	8

[1] Cavalry and H.A. marched at 9 P.M. 16th from Aligunj. Defeate
Holkar at daybreak. Halted two days.

[2] Crossed Jumna at Muttra. Halted three days.

[3] Halted one day.   [4] Halted seven days.

B.

Marches of Major-General Smith from Bhurtpore in pursuit of Amir Khan, 1805.

				Miles
Feb.	8	Muttra	18
,,	9	Ghosna	5 [1]
,,	10	Tochigarh	18
,,	11	Aligarh	25
,,	12	Kamonah	17
,,	13	Panagarh	15
,,	14	Putghat	24
,, ,,	15 16 }	Kamandani	9 [2]
,,	17	Amroka	21
,,	18	Moradabad	20 [3]
,,	20	Rampur	14
,,	21	Chaprah	12
,,	22	Shergarh	12 [4]
,,	25	Mibill	22
,,	27	Moradabad	14
,,	28	Kanat	19
Mar.	1	Badali	13
,,	2	Afzulgarh	13 [5]
,,	3	Sherkot	4 [6]
,,	4	Shergarh	19
,,	5	Moradabad	20
,,	6	Gandghani River	4

[1] Crossed Jumna at Muttra. [2] Crossing the Ganges.
[3] Halted one day. [4] Halted two days.
[5] Left baggage at Sherkot. Battle. Returned to Sherkot after the action.
[6] Halted.

							Miles
Mar.	7	Chandausi	.	.	.	.	25
„	8	Ramgungi River	.	.	.	.	32
„	9	W.N.W. from last camp		.	.	.	20
„	10	Near Sambal	.	.	.	.	18 [1]
„	12	Amroka	.	.	.	.	24 [2]
„	14	Kamandani	.	.	.	.	24 [3]
„	16	Bahadurgunj	.	.	.	.	12
„	17	Takengirabad	.	.	.	.	18
„	18	Kamonah	.	.	.	.	18
„	19	Aligarh	.	.	.	.	18
„	20	Isár	.	.	.	.	21
„	21	Muttra	.	.	.	.	16
„	22	Camp	.	.	.	.	10
„	23	Bhurtpore	.	.	.	.	10

C.

Extract of a Letter dated November 2, 1867, from Colonel Charles P. Kennedy, retired Bengal Artillery, to Captain F. W. Stubbs, R.A.

'In March 1810 (*sic*) the augmented Horse Artillery, three troops, reached Meerut and halted on a bit of lately built jungle ground, where each officer had a bit of land marked off for him to begin building upon, at the commencement of the hot winds.[4] A tiger was killed a few days after within sight of my tent! We had a precious job to build bungalows in the hot winds, and hardly a workman to be had for love or money!'

[1] Halted one day.   [2] Halted one day.
[3] Two days crossing Ganges.
[4] An officer drew tentage allowance. The Government did not provide them with houses; they had to build or rent.

D.

Successive Strengths of a Troop of Bengal Horse Artillery.

—	1804	1809	1818	1825	1827	1845
Captain	—	1	1	1	1	1
Captain-Lieutenant	1	1	—	—	—	—
Lieutenants	3	3	3	3	3	3
Staff Sergeants	2	—	—	1	1	1
Sergeants	5	6	6	6	6	6
Corporals	4	6	6	6	6	6
Gunners, Bombardiers	8	10	10	10	10	10
Matrosses, Gunners	—	80	80	80	80	80
Farriers	1	1	1	2	2	2
Roughriders	1	—	—	2	2	2
Trumpeters	1	2	2	2	2	4
Havildar Lascars	2	1	1	1	1	1
Naicks	2	2	2	2	2	2
Privates	50	24	24	24	24	24
Horses	150	145	165	165	69	169
6-pr. Guns	4	4	4	4	4	4
24-pr. Howitzers	2	2	2	2	2	—
12-pr. Howitzers	—	—	—	—	1835 2	1848 1

E.

Regimental Orders.

BY BRIGADIER N. H. L. SMITH.

Dum Dum, March 10, 1843.

The total absence of official detail on the subject has hitherto prevented the Commandant from noticing the conduct of the late 1st troop 1st Brigade, Horse Artillery, during the insurrection at, and the disastrous retreat from Cabool.

He now publishes extracts from a letter received yesterday from Lieutenant Eyre, late Commissary of Ordnance, as a public record of the high state of discipline and determined bravery exhibited by this gallant and devoted troop on all occasions.

It will always be a subject of sincere gratification to reflect on the noble manner in which they sustained the character of the corps under the severest trial, and in a climate that multiplied a hundredfold the difficulties with which they had to contend, whilst their fate in the unequal struggle demands the deepest sympathy.

Extract from a Letter from Lieutenant V. Eyre, late Commissary of Ordnance in Cabool, to Captain E. Buckle, Artillery Assistant Adjutant-General.

'It is necessary to premise that at the commencement of the rebellion in November 1841 a portion of General Elphinstone's force was sent to occupy the Bala Hissar, and the remainder was concentrated in the cantonment. To the former Captain Nicholl and Lieutenant Stewart were attached with four guns, and to the latter Brevet Captain Waller's detachment with one additional gun, and the troop became equally divided.

'The first active service in the field by the Horse Artillery was on the afternoon of November 3, when a sally was made under Major Loodyne, 5th Native Infantry, and a body of the enemy was defeated, chiefly by the fire of the guns. On this occasion Captain Waller was severely wounded, and from that date up to November 22, when I myself was disabled, the virtual command of the

Horse Artillery detachment in the cantonment devolved upon me; during this period several severe actions took place with the enemy, in all of which our arms were more or less successful. One fort was breached and taken by assault, another was carried by a *coup de main*; and besides several sorties of minor importance two great actions were fought on November 10 and 13 against the collective forces of the enemy, amounting on these occasions to several thousands of horse and foot, in which our side were completely triumphant and two of their guns were captured.

' Provisions, of which there had been from the beginning an alarming scarcity, soon began entirely to fail. The cold of winter set in with unusual rigour; the defence of our long line of low ramparts grievously harassed the troops; the guns placed in battery at the several angles of the cantonment required the constant attendance of the artillerymen, by day and night.

' The gunners from first to last never once partook of a full meal, or obtained their natural rest; of the hardships and privations undergone it would be difficult to convey an adequate idea. During the whole of this most trying period the behaviour of the Horse Artillerymen was distinguished by a degree of patience, cheerfulness, zeal, and fortitude that excited the unbounded admiration of every eye-witness, and filled the hearts of every artillery officer with pride and delight. On November 23 Brigadier Skelton sallied forth with about 700 bayonets and one gun, which (there being no artillery officer available) was commanded by Sergeant Mulhall. An immense army of Afghans poured forth to battle, and a terrible conflict ensued. Sergeant Mulhall and his brave gun's crew committed great havoc amid the deep masses of the enemy, exhibiting a very high degree of professional skill; but their efforts, though partially successful, were ineffectual to repel the overwhelming hosts of assailants. Galled by the fatal fire of the Afghan rifles, the infantry lost heart and fled, leaving our gun to its fate. Staunch to the last, the artillerymen stood by their charge until they were nearly all exterminated; Sergeant Mulhall himself escaping by a miracle, with his clothes perforated with bullets in divers places. In the public report of this day's operations in the field, Brigadier Skelton did ample justice to the artillery sergeant and his devoted little detachment; but the document has, I fear, been lost.

'On December 14, a treaty having been entered upon, our troops were withdrawn from the Bala Hissar, and Captain Nicholl, on arriving in cantonments, requested me to send in a report of the conduct of his men, which I did, but that was also lost in the retreat. That the Horse Artillery sustained their high fame to the last is well known. On the retreat of the army from Cabool, owing to the starved condition of the horses, which disabled them from pulling the guns through the deep snow and rugged mountain passes, the guns were, one by one, spiked and abandoned. In the Khoord Cabool Pass a whole gun's crew perished rather than desert their charge. On reaching Jugdulluck some Horse Artillery-men, headed by Captain Nicholl, acting as dragoons, charged and routed a party of the enemy's cavalry. Throughout the last struggle up to Gandamuck all eye-witnesses concur in testifying to their valour. They died like true soldiers, selling their lives dearly. Only three men escaped with life, being taken prisoners; two others who were left behind with the detachment of wounded at Cabool also survived.'

The above order to be read at a parade of each troop and company in the regiment.

(True extract.)

(Signed) E. BUCKLE.

A.A.-General's Office, Dum Dum, March 11, 1843.

(True copy.)

(Signed) JOHN ANDERSON, Captain,·
Adjutant 1st Brigade Horse Artillery.

Captain Nicholl commanded the above troop for upwards of nine years.

(True copy.)

(Signed) T. NICHOLL, Lieutenant-General, R.A.
(son of the above named).

March 24, 1892.

F.

List of Officers who have served in the Battery.

Year	Captain	Capt.-Lieutenant	Lieutenants			Fire-workers
1801	—	C. Brown	—	M. W. Brown	J. Brooke	—
1802	—	,,	H. Stark	J. Young	—	—
1803	—	,,	,,	,,	—	—
1804	—	,,	,,	,,	W. H. L. Frith	—
1805	—	,,	,,	,,	,,	—
1806	G. Pennington	—	J. P. Boileau	C. P. Kennedy	,,	—
1807	,,	—	,,	,,	,,	—
1808	,,	W. H. L. Frith	H. L. Playfair	,,	W. McQuhae	—
1809	,,	,,	,,	,,	,,	—
1810	,,	,,	G. E. Gowan	,,	,,	—
1811	,,	,,	,,	,,	G. N. C. Campbell	R. S. B. Morland
1812	,,	W. McQuhae	,,	,,	,,	,,
1813	,,		,,	,,	,,	,,
1814	,,	,,	,,	,,	,,	G. Pennington
1815	,,	,,	,,	,,	,,	,,
1816	J. P. Boileau	G. E. Gowan	—	,,	,,	,,
1817	,,	,,	—	F. P. Gowan	,,	,,
1818	,,	—	J. Macalister	R. Roberts	A. Cameron	A. Thompson
1819	,,	—	K. Cruickshank	,,	,,	Lieutenants G. Pennington J. Johnson A. Thompson

Year						
1820	{ T. Nicholl / G. Pennington / A. Thompson / H. Timings / T. B. Bingley / H. Timings / J. Paton }	,,	J. Johnson	,,	—	,,
1821	C. Grant	A. Cameron	J. Johnson	A. Thompson	—	,,
1822	,,	H. Timings	T. B. Bingley	,,	—	T. Lumsden
1823	,,	,,	,,	,,	—	,,
1824	,,	,,	,,	,,	—	,,
1825	F. K. Duncan	,,	C. Grant	G. T. Graham	2nd Captain S. Parlby	,,
1826	T. E. Saye	,,	,,	F. Brind	J. Johnson	,,
1827	,,	,,	A. Humfrays	,,	,,	,,
1828	,,	,,	,,	,,	—	,,
1829	W. C. J. Lewin	W. C. J. Lewin	,,	D. Ewart	W. Bell	,,
1830	D'A. Todd	,,	,,	,,	,,	,,
1831	,,	,,	,,	,,	,,	,,
1832	J. Hotham	W. E. J. Hodgson	,,	,,	—	T. Nicholl
1833	C. Stewart	,,	R. Waller / C. E. Mills	W. Anderson		,,
1834	,,	A. Broome	,,	,,		,,
1835	,,	—	,,	,,		,,
1836			C. Stewart	R. Waller	C. Dallas	,,
1837		A. W. Hawkins	,,	,,	,,	,,
1838		,,	,,	,,		,,
1839		,,	,,	,,		,,
1840					W. S. Pillans	,,
1841						,,

Year	Captain	Capt.-Lieutenant	Lieutenants			
1842	W. Geddes	,,	,,	M. Dawes	,,	R. H. Baldwin
1843	F. Dashwood	,,	V. Eyre	,,	,,	{ A. Wintle
1844	,,	—	J. Mill	,,	W. C. Hutchinson	{ H. Tombs
1845	,,	—	,,	,,	,,	
1846	W. Anderson	R. H. Baldwin	,,	,,	,,	H. T. T. Patterson
1847	,,	,,	,,	H. Tombs	,,	,,
1848	R. H. Baldwin	—	H. Hammond	,,	A. G. Austen	{ J. R. Sladen
1849	,,	—	,,	,,	C. V. Cox	{ H. M. Smith
1850	,,	—	G. Milligan	A. W. Pixley	J. R. Sladen	
1851	,,	—	,,	,,	H. M. Smith	H. M. Smith
1852	,,	—	,,	,,		—
1853	,,	—	,,	,,		T. P. Smith
1854	,,	E. A. C. D'Oyly	D. C. Alexander	,,	,,	A. H. Lindsay
1855	,,	—	,,	A. H. Lindsay	,,	G. B. Traill
1856	,,	—	,,	,,	G. M. Dobbin	{ W. B. Cumberland land
1857	H. A. Olpherts	F. F. Rimmington	G. B. Traill	,,	,,	{ G. B. Traill
1858	,,	—	,,	,,	,,	—
1859	,,	A. H. Lindsay	A. Dixon	C. A. Bayley	G. F. Hamilton	{ G. R. Manderson / A. Dixon
1860	,,	T. P. Smith	,,	,,	,,	{ G. R. Manderson / C. H. Barnes
1861	H. P. de Teissier		,,	,,	,,	—

Amalgamation of the Indian with the Royal Artillery.

Year	Major	Captain	Lieutenants		
1862	H. H. Maxwell, L.C.	T. P. Smith	A. Dixon	C. A. Baylay	G. F. Hamilton
1863	G. A. Renny, V.C.	M. M. FitzGerald	,,		,,
1864				A. Swinton	
1865	J. R. Sladen	,,			
1866		,,	G. F. Blackwood	A. D. Anderson	E. F. Chapman
1867	W. Tod Brown	W. Gully	H. L. Nicholas	,,	,,
1868	,,	A. Douie	,,	,,	,,
1869	,,	E. D. Elliott	,,	,,	
1870					F. S. Loraine
1871	M. M. FitzGerald		J. C. Robson		,,
1872	,,				,,
1873	,,		J. C. Gillespie		,,
1874	,,	M. W. Ommaney		H. J. O. Walker	R. E. Munday
1875	,,	,,	W. Taylor	,,	,,
1876	,,	R. G. S. Marshall	P. Hussey		
1877	,,	,,	R. B. Place	G. H. Mayne	J. R. Jocelyn
1878		,,	P. E. Hamilton	,,	C. M. Western
1879	D. MacFarlan				F. M. Goold-Adams
1880	H. de G. Warter	R. Corbett	,,	F. Beaufort	
1881					
1882	W. R. C. Brough	C. H. Hamilton	J. B. Archdale	J. W. Dunlop	A. C. Bailward
1883	,,		,,	,,	F. J. Murphy
1884		C. B. Coke	,,		
1885	M. R. West	E. Gunner	B. F. Drake	W. V. Faber	G. G. Simpson
1886	,,	,,	,	C. C. Sankey	C. L. M. Knight
1887		,,		A. B. Scott	,,
1888	E. A. Ollivant			,,	

Year	Major	Captain	Lieutenants		
1889	E. A. Ollivant	E. Gunner	B. F. Drake	H. F. Askwith	C. L. M. Knight
1890	,,	H. M. Sandbach	W. D. White-Thomson	,,	,,
1891	C. C. Rich	,,	,,	,,	W. A. Boulnois
1892	,,	,,	,,	G. F. Dixon	,,
1893	,,	E. W. Blunt	,,	,,	H. S. Vallentin
1894	,,	{ T. E. P. Vereker / A. S. Tyndale-Biscoe }	,,	,,	,,
1895	F. Cunliffe	,,	R. St. C. Harman	,,	G. Gillson
1896	,,	,,	,,	,,	,,
1897	,,	A. H. Short	,,	,,	,,
1898	,,	,,	F. W. H. Walshe	A. B. Forman	A. D. Musgrave
1899	,,	,,	,,	,,	,,
1900	C. S. Vores	{ R. Fitzmaurice / Hon. W. O. Sclater-Booth }	G. A. Furse	,,	,,
1901	A. S. Tyndale-Biscoe	H. M. Dawson	,,	W. H. E. Dickenson	H. Bull
1902	,,	A. E. Wardrop	,,	E. W. Browne	,,
1903	,,	Bt.-Major P. Wheatley	,,	,,	,,
1904	,,	,,	,,	,,	,,
1905	C. S. Vores	,,	,,	C. R. Bates	,,

Spottiswoode & Co. Ltd., Printers, New-street Square, London.

Printed in the United Kingdom
by Lightning Source UK Ltd.
113491UKS00001B/274